Usborne

T.Rex
Magic Painting
Book

Illustrated by
Nilesh Mistry

Designed by
Brenda Cole

Dip the brush into
water, then brush it across
the black patterns and lines
within each shape to see
the paint magically appear.

To stop water from
seeping through to the next
page, unfold the flap at the
back of the book and place
it under the page you're
about to work on.